# Rex Runs Away

Betsy Franco
Illustrated by Diane Palmisciano

Pat and Rex are best friends,
and they have lots of fun.

Pat likes to throw the ball,
and Rex likes to catch it.

Rex also likes to run away.
One day Rex dug a hole
under the gate.

"Mom, look at the hole that Rex made.
I need to find Rex and
bring him home," said Pat.

Pat saw Mr. Washington,
the mail carrier, and asked him,
"Have you seen my dog Rex?"

"Yes, I've seen him.
He went that way,"
said Mr. Washington.

Pat stopped in front of the bakery
and asked Linda, the baker,
"Have you seen my dog Rex?"

"Yes, I gave Rex a little bit of bread.
He's a nice dog!" said Linda.
"He went that way."

Pat walked to the pet shop.
"My dog Rex is missing.
Have you seen him?"
Pat asked Mr. Sánchez.

"Rex stopped by," said Mr. Sánchez.

"He's a nice dog.

I saw him go up the street that way."

Pat looked around.
Where did Rex go?

Pat looked down and saw
dog footprints on the sidewalk.
He followed them.

Pat saw Rex at the meat shop.
Mrs. Wong gave Rex a bone.

"You were lots of places!"
said Pat.

"You made friends with everyone!"
he said.
"Everyone likes you."

"But you and I are best friends, Rex," said Pat.

"It's time to go home!"